I Love You, Dad

Conversations with My Father

by
Kenneth James Michael MacLean

I Love You, Dad: Conversations with My Father
Copyright © 2005, 2008 Kenneth James Michael MacLean.
All Rights Reserved

ISBN 13: 978-0-9794304-3-5
ISBN 10: 0-9794304-3-7

Library of Congress Control Number: 2008902147

I Love You, Dad is distributed by:
Baker & Taylor, Ingram Book Group

The Big Picture Press
http://www.kjmaclean.com
kmaclean@ic.net
734 668 0639

Visit us at http://www.kjmaclean.com or
http://www.thevibrationaluniverse.com/
and subscribe to the free Big Picture monthly newsletters.

Typesetting and cover design:
Victor R. Volkman, www.LHPress.com

This is book is dedicated
to those who look
beyond the commonplace.

Table of Contents

Introduction 1
Requiem 3
Thank You 5
Dad Isn't Old Anymore 7
Hanging Out in "Heaven" 9
Life Review 13
New Arrivals 17
A New Relationship: Hell and Purgatory 21
Where is Heaven? 25
Dad Prepares for an Adventure 27
Dad to the Rescue 29
Heaven and Earth and Marty Schottenheimer 31
Father and Son and Family 33
Early Childhood Trauma – Dad Explains Himself 37
"What's it Like To Die?" 41
Dad Sees Through my Eyes 43
Like a Child 45
Guru 47
'All Actions are Motivated by Love' 51
Guardian Angel 55
Incarnation 59
Reincarnating Back on Earth 63
Every Human Being is a Master 69
The Circle of Life: Becoming a Baby Once More 73
The Vortex 77
Heavenly Advice 81
The Power of Consciousness 85
A New Life 89
About the Author 91

Introduction

I had no idea I was about to write this book. I thought I was through with my channeling activities, until my father's death hit me like a ton of bricks. I had been prepared for his passing for a couple of years, but as anyone who has been through the death of a parent will tell you, it simply isn't possible to prepare yourself for the actuality of it.

One day I went out for a walk, trying to overcome my grief, and he was just there.

This book wrote itself. It was actually written by my dad, and I know he gets a great kick out of that. He has a message for all of the readers:

"You are an eternal spirit, and don't let anyone tell you otherwise. There is no reason to fear death. So live! Have fun! Make all your dreams come true, for the end of life always has a happy ending."

Thanks, dad.

Kenneth James Michael MacLean
Ann Arbor, Michigan
December 2005

Note: This book was originally posted in an Internet forum. I have kept that format in order to preserve the spirit in which it was written.

By the way, my dad wants to let you know that he chose the cover for this book.

Requiem

Last night my father died.

Kenneth James MacLean Sr. was born in 1926, in a spiritual dark age between the two world wars, and just before the Great Depression. He was raised in the Catholic Church, which taught him that his soul was irrevocably tainted before he took his first breath. He was placed in military school for two years, where he learned to hate those who disagreed with him. During his 30 years on the Detroit Police force, these ideas were reinforced. He was sometimes an insensitive and bigoted person. He did not come to my wedding because my wife and I were not married in the Catholic Church.

Underneath his gruff exterior, however, was a kind and gentle being who had been taught that the only way a man could truly be a man was to be a tough guy. He often had a kind word for the woman at the checkout counter, the gas station mechanic, or the receptionist at the doctor's office, and he taught me how to do the same. He always taught me to be true to my ideals, and to never back down from them. Because our worldviews were diametrically opposed, however, we did not speak to each other for almost 20 years.

Fortunately, in 1991, we reconciled. I flew out twice to San Diego from my home in Ann Arbor Michigan and we worked it out.

My father had no idea of the true nature of Spirit. He believed that if he did not follow the teachings of the Catholic Church word for word, he would go to hell. He tried many times over the next 14 years to redirect my path back to the church.

I tried to tell him over and over that hell did not exist, that when you leave the body you always go to heaven. His response was, "Well, what's the point of being good then?" I would always say, "Because being good feels better." But he couldn't see that.

During the past year I expected to get a phone call from my stepmother at any time, telling me that he had gone. Two weeks ago on the phone (we always talked on Saturday's at 1:30) he said, "Kenny, I'm ready to go, so don't be surprised." We often talked about the best way to die: you're walking down the hall and you just keel over.

I had imagined having to fly out to California, confronting a man who was terrified of death. I never really believed that a person imprisoned within the beliefs of organized religion could ever find peace. Yet I knew that he had been meditating every day for a year with his rosary.

I received the call from my step-mom last night. "Your father died two hours ago." It was apparent that he had done so quietly and easily. My step mom found him lying on the hallway floor, half in and out of the bathroom. Just as he had called it.

As I write this through my tears, I understand now that despite what you had been taught, dad, you found inner peace. When the true test came, the test of death, you passed with flying colors. You were a true spiritual warrior.

I will never call you again on Saturdays at 1:30, and that makes me cry. I will never hear your voice again, and that makes me cry. And most of all, I will never again hear you say, "You're my number one son," and that makes me cry too.

I'm so, so proud of you Dad. I love you. Thank you for being you, and showing me the way.

Your Number One Son, Ken Jr.

Thank You

Thanks to all who have written me about the death of my father. Your kind words and your healing thoughts are helping me to get through the grieving process.

Dad comes to me when I take my afternoon walk after work. It might seem strange to some to communicate with a dead person. But not to me. I feel him just as strongly as if he were alive and standing right in front of me. If I had any doubts about the spiritual nature of a human being, I don't now.

On Monday I asked him why he was so mean to me when I was a child. He laughed and said, "You know son, you weren't always the son and I wasn't always the father. You didn't do any better than I did!" Dad means that in previous lifetimes our roles were reversed. He didn't believe in past lives when he was alive, but I guess he does now. His snappy retort made me laugh, for it was Ken MacLean Sr. all the way. Let's just say that Dad had a bit of a temper. It didn't take much to get his Irish and Scottish blood boiling.

Yesterday I asked him what he was doing now that he was 'dead.' He laughed and said he was playing cards and drinking beer with departed family members. (My grandma used to have a cottage on Lake Huron and the grownups would do just that).

"But how can you be drinking beer?" I ask. "You're dead!"

"I don't know, son. But I am." He tells me that he feels like a sailor home from a long sea journey. "I'm getting my land legs back. It's going to take some time to adjust to where I am now."

I am full of questions but he doesn't want to talk. I can tell he's really happy though. I told him he could drink all the beer he wanted now, and he laughed (for a good portion of his life, my dad was an alcoholic).

It was good to hear him laugh. His life was so hard and so sad in many ways, but he's released all that now.

And I have to find a way to release my sadness as well. If this keeps up, it won't be too long though. I'm going for my walk in a few minutes and if I hear from him, I'll let you know what he says tomorrow.

Dad Isn't Old Anymore

I can't explain it, but I can just feel him. I have to be in a good mood though, or else it doesn't happen. Today on my walk, I asked him what he was doing and he said, "Catching up with family and friends." He told me just before he died that he was looking forward to seeing departed family members again, and especially his first wife (my mother) who died in 1954.

He doesn't have a lot of time for me today, and basically brushed me off. I got a little angry. Then my mom came in and said "Don't be upset. For the first time in 80 years he's doing something he wants without feeling guilty." My mother died of cancer when I was three years old. She was only 29 years old, but I know it is Lorraine. She feels very warm and loving, but powerful. It's amazing, but this is the first time in my life I remembered being able to talk to my mom and dad at the same time.

The weirdest thing about these "visits" is that my dad doesn't FEEL old! With mom it's different, because she was so young when she left us. But dad feels like a 25 year old. I'm saying to myself, 'It feels odd calling this guy dad. He feels like MY son.' I remember him as an old man, but of course, a spirit does not age, only bodies age. I know that, but it still feels strange.

Actually, it's a BIG comfort to be able to contact him. In three days I have been able to finish my grieving and understand that he is still alive, and he's in a really good place, a place he likes.

So it's really hard to be sad, because I'm grieving for the human expression of my father, who was, at the end of his life, just a shadow of the true being he is now.

I'm looking forward to tomorrow's walk.

Hanging Out in "Heaven"

Almost as soon as my feet hit the driveway pavement, I felt him. He didn't say anything, but waited for me to ask a question.

"Where are you now?"

"I'm still hanging around with the family, especially with your mother."

"What do you do all day? Just float around?"

"We talk, we play cards, we walk, and we play games."

"What kind of games?"

"Vroom! Vroom-vroom!" he says.

"Dad," I say, although this guy seems to be getting younger every day, "what are you doing now?"

"Playing!" he cries, just like a little kid. Apparently, Heaven looks a lot like Earth!

I'm finding it harder and harder to call him dad. Clearly, the 79 year old man I knew, worn down by life, is not who Kenneth MacLean Sr really is. It reminds me of that great movie, *Field of Dreams*, where Kevin Costner's dad comes back as a 25-year-old. Whoever wrote and directed that scene really got it right.

"My name isn't Kenneth MacLean," he says.

"What is it?" I ask.

He sends me something that I can't even put into words. It's more like a feeling.

"If it's OK with you, I'll just keep calling you dad."

"OK, whatever," he says. Kenneth MacLean Sr would never say "whatever," because he believed it was disrespectful. But this guy doesn't have a problem with it.

I'm finding that dad has no interest in metaphysical stuff. I ask him, "Tell me about what your life is like and how you left the body," but he is not interested. He points out that he is like "Dragon," the being in my book *Dialogues: Conversations with my Higher Self*.

"I don't concern myself with deep stuff like that," he says. "I'm a fun-loving guy. I tried to tell you to lighten up and have fun ever since you were a little kid, but you never listened."

Oh that's rich, I think. The policeman and the overzealous Catholic telling me to lighten up! He sticks his tongue out at me and says, "It's still good advice, son."

"OK dad." I feel like I'm a hundred years old compared to him.

I can feel the spirit of my mother now. "Mom," I say, "you told me yesterday that it's possible to have part of you incarnated in a body, and part of you not. How does that work?"

She told me yesterday that when a spirit leaves the body, it achieves a much broader awareness. [Sort of like what happens when you focus light with a magnifying glass into a point. When the magnifying glass is taken away, the light that formed the point is released back into the sea of light that surrounds it. "But you still retain your identity," she says. "You don't turn into an amorphous blob of Oneness. You're still you."]

It's a beautiful day as I walk down the dirt road, and the trees are showing lots of color.

"Imagine yourself outside the body, looking down on it," mom says, so I do. "Now go back in."

"Vroom- vroom. Vroom-vroom."

"Yes dear," says Lorraine, talking to dad.

"If you practice that long enough," mom says, "you'll be able to get out of the body and feel what it's like to go in and come back out."

"Yes," I say, "but when I'm in the body it feels totally solid and real and everything else seems imaginary."

"That's because you haven't fully gotten out yet," mom says. "When you do, you'll feel more like you than ever before, yet you'll still be able to see through the body's eyes."

"Vroom -vroom," dad says. It feels like he's about 11 or 12.

"Dear," mom says to him, "why don't you go to the race track?"

"You mean there's a racetrack around here?" Dad says, astonished.

"Of course!" she says. "You can do anything you want."

Dad disappears. He loved the races and when I was a little kid, would take me to the Motor City Dragway in Detroit, and drink beer.

"He's just like a little boy, isn't he?' I say to mom.

"All men are little boys, son," she says. "Your father more than most." The contrast between mom and dad is startling. Mom feels powerful and deep. Dad feels like a child. "Your father has just arrived," she says. "It's going to take a while for him to get himself together."

I get the feeling of endless excitement, of endless fun and games.

My conception of my father is altering radically. The serious, sad being I knew has totally vanished.

I wonder what my dad will be like tomorrow? If this keeps up, he'll be a little baby!

Life Review

I'm sitting at my computer desk and I feel him. Even though it's been several hours since our last conversation, there seems to be no time gap. It's like he never left.

"Do they really have racetracks up there?" I ask him.

"They've got everything. You just have to know where to find it."

"How do you do that?"

"I don't know," he says. "You just think of it and you're there. When you're new like me, somebody has to show you around though. It's a pretty big place."

"Is it just like earth?"

"It seems like it. But I've only scratched the surface, they say."

I have heard that a recently departed being has a "life review." The being goes over what he or she accomplished in their earthy existence, and the mistakes they made. So I ask him.

"Did you have a life review?"

"Not yet," he replies. "I didn't know you needed one."

"Aren't they mandatory?"

"Not as far as I can tell. I can remember everything that happened to me on earth anyway."

"So you remember every little thing?"

"Yes. Not only about my life, but about all the other ones too."

"Doesn't it give you a headache?" I ask. "Seems like all those memories could be overwhelming."

He laughs. "No, it's like remembering what happened to you yesterday. Except that you can recall every little thing."

"Wow! What were some of your previous lives?"

Dad seems uninterested in that, and changes the subject. There are a lot of people hanging around him. "You remember I told you that your Aunt Myrtle was a schizophrenic?" he asks. "Well, it turns out that she's not such a bad broad after all." (Laughter in background).

Aunt Myrtle says hi.

"We're all watching you Kenny," she says. "You're closer to us than anyone we know."

"What do you mean by that?" I ask.

"You have a feel for what it's like up here," Myrtle says. "Trust your intuition. By the way, we like that book you wrote (Dialogues), but we're a little upset that you didn't ask us anything."

"Yeah, I guess I didn't," I say.

"You went over to the metaphysical group. But we're just as smart as they are."

"Sorry," I say.

"No problem," Myrtle replies. "The next time you have a question, consult us too."

"Dad's not interested."

Laughter. "That's right."

I feel like now is a good time to ask about my occasional struggles with depression.

"Why have I felt depression in my life?' I ask. "And why does it come in cycles?" My life, for the past 35 years, has been 8 or 9 years of joy followed by one of depression. Then the cycle starts over. My doctors haven't got a clue. They recommend drugs, but I'm not a druggie kind of guy. It's not like I'm going to do away with myself or anything, but I'm used to feeling good, and it's irritating.

"You got stuck in your body at an early age," Myrtle says. "It's not important how. Just practice what your mom told you and it should eventually go away."

"Really?" I like that idea.

Dad's back. "Lighten up."

"Yes dad. But it's hard to lighten up when you're physiologically depressed."

Dad ignores that. "I had a good time driving the racecar. And I got to watch some really good dirt car racing."

"Why do you ignore my negative stuff?" I ask.

"Because it's not important," dad replies. "I spent a lifetime doing that and it didn't get me anywhere. I can see that now."

That's good advice. I think I need to listen to my father. He laughs. "I tried to tell you that when I was alive, but you almost never listened."

Sorry, dad.

New Arrivals

Today dad was more subdued than yesterday. He tells me he's still adjusting to his new reality.

I asked him what it was like when he left the body, and he seems willing to answer.

"I can't even remember," he says. "It seems like my earth life was just a dream. I can't even remember who Kenneth MacLean Sr was anymore."

After I question him further, it becomes apparent that he isn't able to recall or feel negative emotion. "I did the best I could in my earth life," he says.

"What's it like up there?" I ask again.

"It looks just like earth except there's even more variety and I can go anywhere I want."

He sees himself in a human body, but mom tells me that it's possible to assume any form you want: animal, insect, whatever. "Once you get the idea that you aren't physical anymore, the sky's the limit," she says.

It's funny but I no longer see my father as a human being. I see him as a pure spirit, and I seem to have lost almost all of my sadness.

"You're feeling sorry for my physical expression," dad says. "But that was only a very small part of me."

I get the impression that a being really can focus part of his or her consciousness in a body, but still have a lot "left over." I have a hard time with this concept, because I see consciousness as a discrete unit, only in association with physical bodies. But it's no big mystery to dad.

"How do you do it?" I ask.

"Don't worry about it son," he says. "You'll find it all out soon enough. Relax and have fun. That's something I was never able to do in my life."

"So when do you stop being human up there?" I ask mom.

She gives the equivalent of a shrug. "Some people never do. Others partake in different realities. We've all greeted your father in human form to ease his transition back to native state." I use the word 'native state' to describe the existence of a pure spirit after he or she leaves the body. I can only get glimpses of what it's like, but one thing is for sure: it's really, really fantastic.

"Is there a special area or place for recent earth arrivals?" I ask.

"Well, most people from earth go to an earth reality, because that's where their attention is. Some people incarnate on earth once or twice, just for the experience. Like going on a scary rollercoaster once to say you've done it. Others get addicted, and come back again and again. There are all kinds of groups up here creating all kinds of realities."

"Have you met anyone from another planet?' I ask mom.

Dad laughs. "Not me. Not yet, anyway." He's looking at me funny. "I had no idea what kind of a person you were, Kenny," he says. "I just wasn't equipped to even remotely understand you when I was on earth."

"Yeah, I knew that."

He says nothing.

"Do you remember when John (my younger brother) told you he was a spiritual being?" I ask him.

Dad laughs. "Yes, I remember that now."

My brother John told me this story ten years ago. When he was 5, he's walking down the street in front of our house and suddenly realizes that he HAS a body, but that he isn't the body. He's excited to tell his dad, because of course, dad is a grown–up and he knows everything. So he runs downstairs. Dad is at his workbench, hammering away.

"Dad! Dad!" Johnny says. "I'm not a body, I'm a spirit!" he says (or something like that).

Dad gives him the weirdest look, like he's some kind of a nut or something. If you knew Kenneth MacLean Sr., you knew that look. It could freeze–dry hell itself. "That's nice," dad says, and goes back to work.

"Right then and there," John tells me, "I sort of figured adults didn't have all the answers."

Dad laughs long and hard. "One good thing about being dead son," he says, "you can't take yourself seriously anymore."

Well, that's something to look forward to, I guess.

A New Relationship: Hell and Purgatory

"We can have a really good relationship now," I tell dad. "I want to know all about what you're experiencing and how you evolve up there."

I figure that might be fun to find out how a "dead" person grows. After all, humans grow and evolve, why not spirits?

"Do you evolve at all, or do you just know everything?"

Dad laughs. "I can tell you I don't know everything son," he says. "But it's interesting: I have the possibility of knowing anything."

"How is that?" I ask.

"There's no money limitations up here. There's no physical limitations either. You do have to know about something before you can go there though."

"You know I really like you," I say. There's something about my dad that is really beautiful. It feels like he's a part of me.

"I love you too," he says. "I'm so glad I was able to tell you that when I was on earth."

Dad used to end all of our conversations by telling me he loved me. That was pretty cool, even though sometimes I didn't really believe it. But now I know it was genuine, and that feels good.

"Do you have rest periods up there?"

"No son. There's no resting. I don't have time for that, because I don't get tired anymore. Everything is so exciting."

"I just can't get over the idea that where you are is just like earth."

Dad doesn't know what to say, other than, it's pretty obvious to him. He doesn't know anything else, and so his perception of reality matches the reality he has within his consciousness.

"I don't know how you know all this stuff," dad says. "You're like some kind of guru or something."

I laugh, embarrassed. "I don't know whether I'm imagining this or if it's real," I say.

"Of course it's real!" he says, offended. "You don't get to dismiss me just because I'm not physical anymore!"

Right dad. I guess that was pretty insulting.

"Don't worry about it, kid. I don't get angry anymore like I used to on earth."

"Why did you get so angry?" I ask.

"Because I always thought there was a right way and a wrong way. And I saw so many people going the wrong way."

Dad makes complicated things simple. I already mentioned how his military school training, his religion, and his work on the police force all led him to one way of thinking.

"So there's no wrong or right?" I ask.

Dad pauses. "I wouldn't say that." For the first time I feel a little of that KJ MacLean Sr. energy. "It's better to help someone than to kill him," he says. If he had a head, he'd scratch it. "But I guess there really isn't a wrong way, is there? If people always wind up in this place, then even killing isn't wrong."

That's what I tried to tell him before he died.

"Is there a hell?" I ask. "Or a purgatory?"

Dad thinks about that for a while. "I don't know, son. Maybe there is. That's what keeps me from really believing that there isn't wrong and right. I don't know enough yet to answer that. Besides, if there is a hell, I'm not interested in investigating it. I spent too much time in sadness when I was on earth to even want to find out."

It's interesting. Dad still feels like dad, but without the negative stuff attached. He seems to be more introspective when talking with me tonight, less like a little kid.

"That's because you need to lighten up!" he says brightly. "You're getting to be a bummer. Let's talk about something cheerful!"

"I think I'm done." I say. "I'll talk to you on my walk tomorrow."

Dad smiles and I feel a big wave of love. "I'll be looking forward to that," he says.

So will I.

Where is Heaven?

"I'm feeling a little lonely today Dad," I say. I try my trick of imagining myself outside the body, and connecting to spirit. I find a little relief there.

"You're thinking of heaven as "up there" and it isn't," he says. "It's all around you."

"Huh?"

"I didn't 'go' anywhere when I died," Dad says. ""I'm just experiencing things from a different perspective."

I don't really understand that, but it's OK. "It's really fun to be able to feel your energy," I say. "I'm really grateful. I never realized how important you were to me," I say, my eyes tearing up a little.

'"Woman!" he says cheerfully. "Stop crying! I never understood why women cry when they're happy."

Yes dad.

My dad is so very wise in some ways, and so dumb in others. He laughs. "It doesn't matter now. We can communicate with our barriers down now."

I'm so thankful for that. Just to feel the true "dad" bucks me up. I'm still recovering from my illness and sometimes I feel down, but dad picks me right back up again. Thank you dad.

Dad Prepares for an Adventure

Today the whole family was gathered around dad. I asked him what was going on and he said, "I'm going on an adventure."

"Adventure?"

"I don't understand what's going to happen, but it's going to be interesting."

It feels like the time I was a kid and dad woke me up at 5AM to tell me that the whole family was going to drive across country from Michigan to San Diego. Back in 1962, that was a big deal.

I can feel his excitement.

Dad feels bigger today, less like a little kid (although that's still there) but more now like ...God.

Mom explains. "Your father is discovering himself. When you first come back from earth, you don't remember your full capabilities."

I ask her to explain.

"When you're human, you only have 5 senses. But when you are non-corporeal, you have lots more. Dad is learning to use those now."

"What's it like?" I ask.

There is a little sadness. Not much, but a little. "I can't explain that to you son," she says. The family, my mom, dad, uncles and aunts, all feel like huge, magnificent beings. I am a little baby in comparison. The grownups are about to go on a journey that the child cannot take. "Your spiritual sensors can't be described in language, because there are no reference points for them. But it's going to be exciting."

"I'll tell you when I get back Kenny," he says.

It's been 6 days since dad 'died.' Eleanor Martin, my mom's mother, says, "Your father was taught that God was an unreachable, Supreme and powerful Being, and that a human being was a nothing, an insignificant speck, trying to be worthy of God's love. It's taken him a while to understand that he IS God."

Dad smiles. "It's still hard for me," he says, "but I'm getting used to it. They tell me it's time for me to spread my wings a little."

I can't tell you how eager and excited he is.

"When will you leave?" I ask.

"When we're ready, son. Time doesn't pass for us like it does for you. We might still be here when you take your walk tomorrow."

It is becoming clearer to me that the earth reality my father is in is just a sort of way station. Not a way station exactly, because lots of souls hang out there. But it's similar to entering the foyer of a house. You don't usually hang out in the foyer, even though you can get a view of both the inside of the house and the outside world.

"Tell me as much about it as you can, OK?" I ask, a little afraid that he might disappear on me forever.

"Don't worry. I'll always have a part of me available to talk to you," he says.

Wow. He's growing faster than I can comprehend.

Now I understand why my wife can never feel her mother. She probably took off into some other, I don't know, spiritual reality that has nothing to do with earth. I'm getting the idea that the universe of experience is so vast that it's infinite. Or so big that a human being can't comprehend it, anyway.

I'm a little sad that Dad is becoming something much greater than I can comprehend. But he seems so happy, how can I feel uncomfortable?

Dad to the Rescue

Last night I woke up from a dream in which my father was trying to show me how to do something. As a child, I was a big disappointment to him. He played football and was an all–city running back in a Detroit high school. Dad was great with his hands, and could fix anything. In short, he was just what any guy should aspire to be. But he got a son who was like his wife: intelligent, sensitive, and uninterested in guy things (except sports). I liked to read and was forever trying to figure out the answer to questions like "Why are we here?" and "What is life?"

Dad had no patience for that stuff.

Anyway, in the dream he was instructing me to do something very complicated with a furnace (don't ask me why, dreams are that way sometimes), and as usual, I couldn't get it. He became exasperated as always, and I woke up feeling panicked. I felt like I was tumbling down into a black pit, spinning out of control. It was terrible, but it's been a recurring feeling my entire life. But I felt Dad right there and he said, "I love you son." He showed me some incidents when, as a very little child, he got mad at me. For him this was no big deal, for dad could get violently angry and the next second it would be gone. But as a little child, I became terrified, and overwhelmed. He showed me how these incidents gradually built up into horrible feelings. When they come, I am completely powerless, depressed, and I don't feel like life is worth living. Anybody who's human has probably experienced something like it. But dad guided me through it this time and helped me turn these ghastly vibes into more loving vibes. He told me that he loved me over and over, and showed me two incidents that really made me feel a lot better.

One was when I was a little baby, and Dad held me in his arms. He smiled down at me with the most complete feeling of love. I have to say that until the age of 47, I never heard him once tell me he loved me. I never once saw him smile lovingly at me. He was too conflicted for that. I needed it, but I never got it. But now, as a baby in my father's arms, it just felt so perfect.

In the next incident, I am sitting in a wooden high chair. I can't be more than 6 or 7 months old. I am slapping my hands happily down on the wooden table, and giggling. Dad is spooning some baby food into my mouth and I am gurgling. Sometimes I let it roll down my chin because it feels so delicious. I am happy and smiling and so is Dad.

These are wonderful gifts because I remember almost nothing of my life before the age of 5. It helps to ease the pain. It helps me to understand that my dad was a wonderful person who never recovered from the death of his first wife, and kept the emotions of guilt, anger and unworthiness bottled up inside him for over 50 years.

But with his help, I am exorcizing my own demons. It's so great to have someone who can always be there if I need him.

He tells me that he can always come back into the 'foyer' and talk, even if he's off in never–never land somewhere, and that makes me feel really good.

Heaven and Earth and Marty Schottenheimer

The afternoon is sunny, the temperature about 43 degrees Fahrenheit. The Fall colors are in full bloom, and the sun peeps out behind a cloud, sending yellow rays of illumination over the pleasant neighborhood scene. All of a sudden I feel my father there with me, looking through my eyes.

"Isn't it beautiful?" he said.

It was, I replied. From him I received a rush of joy and well–being. For him, it was like returning to a well–loved place. "I'm addicted to this place," he said, meaning earth. "There are so many exciting places to visit in heaven, but I always come back here eventually," he says. "It's home."

Dad can perceive through me at will, apparently, but I cannot follow him on his journeys.

"Here is where the action is," he says. "Earth, I mean."

He tells me he will probably spend a lot of time in the 'foyer,' my nickname for the non–physical environment that closely matches earth reality. Of course, things are a lot easier 'up there' than down here. "No death or taxes!" Dad opines cheerfully.

"Do you plan on returning to earth soon?' I ask.

"Not for a little while," he says. "I'm enjoying myself right now." From the sidebands of his thought I gather that there is some sort of system of incarnation to earth, but he's not interested in talking about that right now.

It feels like dad is almost fully adjusted to his new existence. He sent me some pictures of where he'd gone on his 'adventure.' One of them was a world of pure light; others were incomprehensible to me. Apparently there really is life on other planets out there in the big wide universe, and there are groups of souls who like to hang around in the environments associated with those planets. Dad went to visit some of these places.

Later that afternoon I'm watching a football game (San Diego Chargers vs. Philadelphia Eagles). In the final two minutes, San Diego is just about to kick a field goal that will give them a 7 point lead. But the Eagles block the kick and run it back for a touchdown to take a 3 point lead. I feel dad right there with me. He was a big Chargers fan. "Typical," he says, metaphorically shaking his head. After Philadelphia kicks off, the Chargers march down the field. There is a little over a minute left. Drew Brees passes for a 23 yard gain down to the Eagles' 20 yard line. The Chargers will be nicely set up for a touchdown try, or at the very least, a tying field goal, but the San Diego receiver has the ball taken out of his hands, and the Eagles recover the fumble. Dad laughs. "That's Marty Shottenheimer to a T," he says. "Something always goes wrong." Dad always complained about Marty–ball when he was alive, and apparently things haven't changed now that he's 'dead!'

Father and Son and Family

At first dad wasn't very communicative, or else I wasn't receiving him very well. It's almost as if his energy, or personality, is becoming integrated with my own. That is to say, I don't perceive him as a totally distinct personality anymore, but more as a blend of himself and Spirit.

"Hey, wait a minute," he says. "I'm still me, I'm just not the hard–nosed bastard I used to be." He laughs when he says this.

"So why do I feel you differently?" I ask.

"Because so much of what I used to be was not who I really am now," he says, smiling lovingly.

That seems right to me. Dad seems to have completely left behind all that nasty stuff.

"You know," he says, "You never understood me either. Understanding works both ways."

That's true, I think. I blamed a lot of our family difficulties on my father, but I never took the time to understand him. "But isn't it the duty of the parent to understand the child?" I ask.

"Of course," he says, "but it takes two to tango, as your grandma always used to say."

Dad's comments are helpful. I realize that even though I'm almost 54 years old, I have viewed myself as a victim in our relationship, even though he moved to San Diego in 1972.

"I never could have heard that from you when you were alive," I say. "It would have just pissed me off."

"One of my biggest frustrations in my earth life was my inability to express myself to the family," he says, very animated. "I wanted to have a big happy family, but I wasn't happy myself. All of my personal garbage got twisted up inside me, and it just wouldn't come out right."

I can see that now Dad's anger was partially a result of his frustration in that regard. He simply was not capable of expressing his feelings, even though he wanted to.

"That's right," he says. "Now you're beginning to understand me."

"But I don't have to understand the *you* that you were," I object. "As you said, all that stuff wasn't really you."

"Yes, you do," he replies. "For your own peace of mind, you have to make peace with the guy I was, the guy that was your father. If you don't, a part of you will always remain twisted too."

Wow, that's really deep, I think. "Thanks Dad. I'll have to give that some thought."

"The old man isn't so dumb after all, is he?"

I laugh. He used to say that to me when he was alive. But he's right. I have to resolve my own anger with the former personality that was my father.

In these conversations I am learning that Spirit truly exists. The idea that 'you only go around once in life' seems really stupid now.

Tonight I went to a concert at historic Hill Auditorium in Ann Arbor. The University of Michigan symphony orchestra played Beethoven's 9th symphony. For the third movement, the orchestra was joined by the UMS Choral Union, around 200 voices. The concert was a celebration of the 125th birthday of the university's school of music, known as one of the top institutions of performing arts and music in the world.

The symphony was in top form, and the third movement was especially inspiring. I was so juiced leaving the concert that I hopped down the stairs two at a time.

Dad showed up halfway through the second movement. He loved classical music, but always looked on Ann Arbor as a "hippie town, full of liberals." Well, dad sure was blown away tonight.

I learned tonight that he would have been unable to enjoy the concert without perceiving it through me. Apparently, non–corporeal spirits aren't able to "vibe down" to the physical level. I thought that was interesting.

Early Childhood Trauma – Dad Explains Himself

The day is blustery and cold. The wind is gusting around 40 mph and the temperature is in the low 40's.

As I start my walk I don't feel him anywhere. Then I begin to think about what he said yesterday. That I have to make peace with the person he was in his earthly life.

"But how do I do that?' I say out loud.

Then I feel him. "You have to find something about me that you can admire," he says.

That's easy. As I mentioned before, Dad always had a kind word for strangers. "But why," I ask him, "could you be nice to strangers, but not to your own family?"

"Because it was easy to be nice to people I didn't know," he replies. "It was impossible to be nice — except occasionally — to family. It reminded me of my failures as a person and as a father."

I can feel from him that it had something to do with his feelings of guilt about Lorraine's death, and his alcoholism.

I bring up an incident that happened when I was about 2. I innocently toddled into my parents' bedroom one night when mom and dad were having sex. Dad went ballistic and grabbed me. He was yelling at me, and mom was freaking out. Dad being dad, he quickly calmed down and put me back in my crib. It was his old Irish temper asserting itself, and quickly subsiding. For Lorraine, however, it was an epiphany. For her, having led a sheltered life, her illusions about her husband were shattered. They had been having a tough go of it anyway, and she had already called her parents, wanting to come back home, but her father told her she had to stick it out. Anyway, she came into my room and held me in her arms and, in the way mothers have with little children, I could feel exactly what she felt. She made the decision right there to quit living. It took her another year to contract the disease (leukemia) that would kill her, but it was all over right then.

I ask dad whether that incident was true or not. He said, "Something like that." It was the source of his guilt for the rest of his life, for he felt that he was partly responsible for his wife's death.

"You see Kenny, your mother gave up on our marriage after that, and her family as well. It was my big secret. Every time I saw a member of our family (which was every day, of course) it just reminded me of my guilt."

"But why didn't you unburden yourself?" I ask. "Get some therapy, or at least go to confession?"

"What difference would that have made?" he replies. "What was done, was done."

"Yes, but it could have made you feel better," I say.

He tells me that his religion told him that sinners have to suffer. And so he suffered. His military school training told him that he had to be a man and solve his own problems, and not be a burden to others. And so this beautiful soul was trapped. He could not give the love he felt to his family, but found an outlet, albeit briefly and occasionally, with strangers.

Now I understand the earthy persona that was my father a lot better. It's a great relief to me. As I walk along the dirt road, I look across the farmer's field off to my left and I see a metal electrical tower on Pontiac Trail, a mile away in the distance. I feel an expansion of my awareness, and suddenly realize that my father spent his whole life holding himself in. And I have spent a lot of my life doing the same. I could never understand my father, and I never tried. I just resisted him and what he stood for. But as I opposed him, I also opposed myself, for a part of him has always been in me.

I'm beginning to see the light. Better late than never, I guess.

"What's it Like To Die?"

I ask Dad what it was like to die.

He says he could feel just when it was going to happen, and he felt no fear. "It was exciting," he says. "I knew I was going to meet up with the family."

"Where did you go?" I ask.

"I didn't go anywhere," he says. "It's not like on earth, where you jump into your car and travel in time and space. Although at first it did feel like I was going somewhere. Now I realize I'm just seeing differently."

I ask him to tell me more. "Well, in the first place I never looked back at the body. It was old and uncomfortable and I was glad to leave it. I had, as you know, already decided to have it cremated. Right after I left the body, I found myself in a house that looked like Grandma Martin's. The family was there, and everyone greeted me. I felt so happy!"

"Did the physical universe just fade out when you left the body?"

"I don't know what you mean," he says. "I found myself in a new place, that's all."

"Do you still see yourself with a body?" I ask.

"When I first arrived, yes. Now I understand that it's possible to change the way you think about yourself."

Dad becomes a bird, soaring. As I walk along, I receive an impression of what that feels like. I feel my awareness expand upward to the sky, with its white tufts of clouds, and the sun peeping through.

"Wow, that's amazing," I say.

"That's how it is all the time here," he says.

Dad is totally comfortable now. He feels less like Kenneth MacLean Sr and more like me. Or more like some sort of generic angel.

"There's a feeling of love that permeates this place," he says. "I'm just soaking it up."

"Why is there so much misery on earth?" I ask.

He laughs. "Mankind is good at denying his true nature," he responds. "Religion is the primary culprit. At least it was for me."

Heresy, I think. Dad would never have thought that when he was alive.

"I did think about it son," he said. "But I never could abandon my faith. And it helped me to find peace at the end."

"So it's all good," I say.

"It's all good for me, anyway," he says selfishly. "I'm enjoying myself, just knowing that it's impossible to feel miserable."

I don't know how many more of these conversations we're going to have. But he tells me I can always call on him whenever I need him.

"I'm going to do that," I say. "I've never had anyone to mentor me, at least no one who understood me."

"All right then," he says, and I don't feel him anymore. I think he's hanging around primarily for my benefit.

Wherever he is, he's got a life to enjoy, and he's really thrilled about it. I'm kind of sad I can't participate in that life, because it feels so immensely exciting, but he assures me that I can be just as happy on earth as he is in heaven.

Maybe we'll talk about that tomorrow.

Dad Sees Through my Eyes

At first dad did not want to talk.

"Let me see through you," he says. "Try to feel how it feels to me."

We walked for about 5 minutes. The fall colors are bright, the temperature is cool, and the sun shines through another mostly cloudy sky. It is clear that dad hasn't a care in the universe. He is not worried about anything. He exists completely in the now, and he encourages me to do the same.

I sure would like to. "Every time I try to do that, other thoughts come into my head," I say. "And some of them are negative."

He ignores my negative statement, sighing with pleasure. It's the only thing I feel irritated with him about. He utterly refuses to acknowledge my pessimism.

"The earth is a beautiful planet," he says, just enjoying the view through my eyes. "There's something about being here in a body that is...just different. Different in a good way."

"How do I get to the place where you are?" I ask. "I would love to forget about the mortgage and the bills and the war in Iraq..."

"Look son," he says. "It's real simple. Just make a wish, and then don't worry about it."

"Easy for you to say," I say. "You couldn't do it when you were alive," I accuse.

Dad smiles. "That life is behind me now. I never think about who I was, only about who I am now."

"You have no excuse, son," he says, after a pause. "You know what the score is. You know how the system works. I didn't have that advantage."

I agree. I even wrote two books on 'how it works. but I know that I can't always practice what I preach. "Why is it so hard then?" I ask.

"Because you make it hard. That's the answer."

Through my eyes Dad sees a bird flying high above the cornfield. He immediately begins to soar, and I receive a delicious feeling of freedom. For an instant, I am the bird. It's astonishing.

"Oh, how I'd like to be able to do that!" I exclaim.

Dad smiles. He's doing that a lot now. "It works the same for me as it does for you," Dad says. "I can just think about something now and have it happen. It took me a while to remember how to do it, I admit. But if you want something and don't make up reasons why it can't happen, you'll get it."

"Anything?"

"Anything." Dad is completely certain of that. I wish I had his confidence.

As I walk along, I feel my father around me, inside me, excited and joyful. I understand that there is nothing preventing me from feeling like this all the time. Only the prison of my own self-limiting beliefs.

I can't tell you how good it feels to be able to contact my "real" father. I love you, Dad.

"I love you too, son."

It's interesting that I only feel him when I'm really peaceful, or when I'm really excited. The walks are a very peaceful time for me, especially when the weather is so nice. The concert on Tuesday was inspirational. I suddenly realized that when I'm inspired, I'm in the now. Apparently we can't connect unless I'm in the now. I guess he's there all the time.

Lucky guy!

Like a Child

Today as I began my walk, I wasn't thinking about dad. I felt tired, probably because I had stayed up late the entire week watching the World Series.

After a couple of minutes, I felt him. I don't have a lot of questions anymore. He's answered all of them now. I feel like I understand who he was when he was my father, and I understand even better who he is now.

The day is cold, the sun obscured behind the clouds. I have to wear an extra layer of clothing today. The long Michigan winter is almost upon us. My thoughts turn away from the scenery and inward, but Dad doesn't want that. "Let's enjoy the view," he says, and so I place my eyes on the road, and the colorful trees. The sky is especially beautiful today, he says. There are large white rows of clouds floating in a bowl of intense blue. Dad sighs with pleasure and I get a surge of energy. There is no conversation, just being.

At about the 3/4 mark, I begin to think about myself and who I am. I think about my life and especially my childhood. I feel sort of innocent and cute and sweet, almost like a puppy, or a kitten. I am definitely not a tough guy. Dad wouldn't like that at all, I think to myself. Suddenly, Dad says, "Right there, that's who you are, son. You've been resisting that for a long time. And so did I."

It is a revelation to me. Could it really be? I wonder. As if in answer, the sun breaks through the clouds and shines warmly upon the landscape, sending its bright yellow light everywhere. I feel a rush of well-being. "Yes, that's you," he says. It's true, and it feels right. "I helped to destroy that within you when I was alive," he says, "just as I had it destroyed within me. Now I can help restore you to yourself."

I recognize that innocence within him now. As I look back over his life, I can see how he kept his own light well-hidden. It was something he knew he had to do. It was his duty, he thought, to be strong and manly and tough, and like a good soldier, he performed his duty to the best of his ability. But now he's free, and he's helped to make me a little freer as well.

Is this the end of our talks? I don't know. He feels almost like a part of me now, and I seem to be able to call on him whenever I want. We'll see what happens tomorrow.

Guru

Today is gorgeous — a clear blue sky and the colors are magnificent. I can feel my father walking with me, and our rapport is now at such a level that conversation is at a minimum. We are just being together.

I wonder when my body will fully recover its vitality, and why I managed to hurt my back again two months ago. Dad gently says, "Questioning why and how will only stick you where you don't want to be," he says. He gently guides me to a feeling of well being about my body. "Keep your thoughts there," he advises

Dad is now a true mentor. It's something I always wanted as a child, but it didn't happen. Dad believed in corporal punishment, and strict obedience. He dominated the family with his personality and his uncompromising attitude. I learned early on in my life that my opinions were unwanted. It's funny. Dad wanted an adventurous son, but acted in a way which made that difficult.

"You didn't have to obey me," he says. "You had the choice to be your own man."

"Right," I say. "When I did try to be my own man, you'd beat me with a belt or an electrical cord. I was just a kid."

Dad smiles. "Nevertheless, you could have done. Many boys do, you know." He does not apologize.

I think about that for a while. There is definitely a feeling of victimhood associated with my childhood. "That feeling is what is holding you back," he says. "What's done is done. Keep your eyes on your goals."

As I walk along I realize that he is right. That stuff happened almost 50 years ago! It's time to let ALL of it go.

"Now you're talking, son," he says benevolently. "When you die, you naturally release your issues. It's like taking out the trash — all of your personal garbage goes away. It's like magic. But don't wait like I did until you die. Have fun now!"

That's good advice, but how do I do that?

"There you go again," he says. "Your how's and why's always stick you back in your shit."

"But it's fun to figure out the how's and why's!" I say.

"Yes, but if you try to figure out the reason for something that's bothering you, you just stick your face in it," he says. "You wrote a book about that."

Yup. I did. But…but…

Dad grins. "You were always the smart one," he teases. "Now I'm the guru and you're the dummy."

Why is it so easy to give advice about someone else's problems, but so much harder to handle your own?

Dad laughs. "All of us up here are experts," he says. "Do you know why?"

"No, why?"

"Because none of us has any problems! So we can always give perfect advice about yours." He's laughing. "Don't worry son, what seems to you to be a big deal will turn out to be much ado about nothing," he says. "I know it doesn't feel like that now, but believe me, when you get up here it's just a walk in the park!"

I can feel his excitement, his sense of well being. He is totally free, and it feels so great. I long for that.

"You're on the rollercoaster called earth," dad says. "Enjoy it! I've been looking over my life and even though I felt miserable most of the time, I understand now that I would never change a thing."

"You mean you'd rather be miserable than happy?" I reply.

"No, dummy! I mean that now, from my superior viewpoint, I can really appreciate what I went though. And so will you."

Then he's gone.

I think he's got some explaining to do.

'All Actions are Motivated by Love'

"So explain this idea that you wouldn't change a thing about your miserable life." It's two days later, but we pick up right where we left off. It's as if no time has passed.

I feel a rush of love. "What I mean is that no matter how bad it gets, there's a happy ending."

My wife Jenny would like that idea. She refuses to read books or watch movies that don't end well. "Life throws us enough crap," she says. "I don't want it in my entertainment too."

"That's a smart wife you've got there son," Dad says. "You might want to pay more attention to her."

"Oh, I do," I say, and he laughs. He always used to say that a successful relationship between a man and a woman is based on the idea that the woman is always right.

"When you die," he says, continuing with the previous thread, "and look back on your life, you only remember the good parts."

"How does that work?"

He metaphorically scratches his head. "I don't know. All I know is that right now, I'm incapable of experiencing anything negative. So when I look back over my life, it all seems worthwhile."

"I'm having trouble understanding that," I say. "If you're miserable your whole life, then there aren't any good bits."

He pauses and thinks. "I'm trying to figure out the best way of explaining this to you," he says. "For example, remember the time you came home from college and I was drunk?"

"Yeah I remember that." Dad was wailing on my step mom and the house was filled with some pretty bad vibes. I couldn't wait to get out of there.

"When I look back over that now, I can fully understand my motivations for doing what I did. I was so frustrated with my inability to express my love for my family, and so tired of my pain, that I lashed out at the ones I loved most. Underneath my actions and my negative emotions, believe it or not, was a powerful feeling of love that I couldn't express. You see Kenny, what I've learned since I died is that EVERY action, no matter how horrible, is motivated by that feeling of love." He gets kind of starry-eyed and says, "It's amazing. I never could have understood that when I was alive, but it seems so obvious to me now."

"But how can torture and murder be motivated by love?" I ask.

"I'm not a philosopher, son," he says. "I don't have any fancy explanations for you. But I can tell you unequivocally that underneath every single action, no matter how heinous, is love. The greater the hate, the greater the love that lies behind it."

Wow. I don't understand, but it sounds good! It's just the opposite of what my religion taught me.

"So, have you met Hitler yet?" I ask.

I told him when he was alive that Adolf Hitler went to heaven, just like Mother Theresa, but he never believed me.

"Haven't seen him, don't want to," he says. "But I'd imagine that Hitler had the same problem I had. He just expressed his frustrations on a bigger stage."

I shake my head. "Maybe I'll understand when I die, but I don't now."

He smiles. "Well, that won't happen for a while yet," he says.

"You mean you can tell when I'm going to die?" I ask.

"I can tell that you're not going to die any time soon," he says.

"How?"

"There is a vortex of potential that surrounds every person," he says. "Even though you've been thinking about death a lot lately, it's not in the cards for you yet." He raises his hands. "Don't ask me how I know. I just know. I can see it, and it's not possible to explain how."

I like the idea of life always having a happy ending, but it sure would be nice to have things perfect NOW, when I'm still alive. Somehow I don't think Dad has the answer to that one.

Guardian Angel

My father has become like a personal guardian angel to me. When I ask for him, he's there. When I'm feeling down, he nudges me toward the positive. Dad is totally free now, and that makes me really happy.

My step–mom called me yesterday. She's still grieving, but it does not seem real to me that dad is dead. As I've said before, he's a lot more real to me now than he ever was. I tell my step–mom about our conversations, and she accepts it. Pretty amazing.

I know for certain now that death is a myth. There is no death, just a transition of consciousness from one plane of existence to another. The glimpses I get of my father's reality are fascinating. If you've ever seen the movie "Made in Heaven" it's a little like that, except that there is no requirement to incarnate on earth.

Apparently, earth is just one of an almost infinite number of realities available to experience. Dad remarks that once you have a lifetime on earth, however, it gets addicting. Sort of like the explorer who made a solo journey to the South Pole. I heard an interview with this guy on Fresh Air with Terry Gross several years ago. During the voyage, he had a number of near death experiences but seven years later he was considering another trip. Terry was astonished. "But why?" she asked, and he basically said that he had never felt so alive during his journey, and his normal life now seemed boring. According to dad, the earth experience is often like that: incredibly intense. When it's good it's really good and when it's bad it's really bad. "That's why we only go for about 80 years," he says. "I'm glad I got off that rollercoaster."

He brings up a topic that he would never discuss in his earth life: sex. "A lot of us go to earth just for sex," he says.

"Why?" I ask.

"Because in many cultures — including the United States — sex is proscribed. War, death, poverty, all these things are accepted, but the unclothed human body is considered inappropriate or even sinful."

"So what makes sex so special then?"

"Precisely because society forbids it. If people simply ran around naked, it wouldn't be nearly such a thrill. Besides," he says, "the human body is really very ingeniously designed. Physical sex can be an incredible high, especially when it is accompanied by a feeling of love. Physical sex is actually designed to stimulate the feeling of love, which is why it is so beneficial."

"You were against sex when you were alive," I point out.

"I was confused," he replies. "But not any more!"

I feel a rush of youthful energy. I still haven't entirely gotten used to the idea that he isn't still an old man. He's also much wiser and more knowledgeable than he was .even last week.

"The human experience is designed to allow a being to experience as a helpless child, a teenager, a middle aged person and an old person, all in one short lifetime. It's totally awesome!" he says.

"Are you thinking of coming back already?" I ask, astonished.

"Well, I sort of am," he says.

"But you just got there!"

"It's not like that, son," he says. "I've already experienced what you might call several lifetimes here. On earth, time is rigid, and demarcated. There's a clock on every wall. Day turns into night and back to day again, providing everyone with the same reference points. It's not like that here. I can't explain it, but I've done so much already."

He sends me a 'thought packet' that I have to unwrap. It contains thoughts, feelings and experiences all rolled up into a ball. He sends me an image of himself in a balloon, floating serenely in a beautiful blue sky. Then he sends me an image of himself in a whitewater kayak, going 50 miles an hour and fighting to keep his kayak from smashing into huge rocks.

"That's the difference between heaven and earth," he says.

"I've had enough excitement," I said. "I'll take the balloon ride."

"It all depends on your perspective," he says. "I felt the same way as you, but now it's different."

I didn't think we were going to have any more of these conversations, but I guess I was wrong!

Incarnation

"How do people incarnate on earth?" I ask. "What if there are more who want to come than there are bodies to go around? Is there some kind of lottery?"

Dad laughs loud and long.

"No, you're a little confused on that," he replies. "There is never any conflict." He sends me an image of a fountain of water flowing into a number of smaller basins. "The water just flows into the basins, and is recycled back. It's effortless."

"Yes, but we're talking about conscious personalities, not water," I object. "Unless you're saying that we're all just one big glob of Oneness."

He smiles. "When consciousness becomes associated with a body, only a part of you is in there. Any one of us can look through your eyes and experience through you. What I'm saying is that we ALL get to experience what you experience."

I'm trying hard to grasp this. "You mean that human beings are just little receptacles for non–physical consciousness to experience through? So you guys are like parasites, piggy–backing on top of us?"

He laughs. "We don't see it like that. Consciousness isn't like a piece of matter that can only occupy one point in space at a time. We can be anywhere we wish, at any time."

That blows my mind. "If all of you are looking through me, how come I can't feel you?"

"Because all of you are so into what you're doing. That's one of the attractions of earth, as I've already explained. Another reason is that we don't experience your negative emotions. We're always on such a high level of joy and love that most humans can never reach. You only feel us during your moments of pure joy and love."

Again I am reminded that the human being I knew as 'dad' has morphed into something much grander and wiser. But I still feel him as my father, so I'll continue to use that term to describe him.

"So what's the point of being human if it sucks so badly?"

He shrugs. "It's *different*. And it's different in such an astounding way that we can't resist coming back again and again. Also," he adds, "when you regain the full knowledge of who you are, you understand completely that there is no possibility of failure. You're eternal and immortal and your fundamental nature is one of eagerness, excitement, and joy. That's just the way it is Kenny, and when you realize that fully it just makes you feel so wonderful that I can't even describe it. And so we come back for another physical experience, and another, and another."

"Are there some beings who have never had a physical incarnation?"

"Your question doesn't make a lot of sense," he says. "Remember that we can all perceive through you, so we can all experience the physical."

"Yes," I say, "but there is one very important difference: you don't experience the lower emotions. And that's the greatest part of being human."

"That's true," dad says cheerfully, "but how much misery you experience as a human being is entirely up to you! No one forces you to resist your inherent nature. Believe me, the only time you can be sad, or angry, or irritated, is when you begin to question your innate goodness. That, and that only, is what causes you to feel the lower emotions."

"You're kidding," I say drolly. "So all the murder, poverty, war and misery we see around us has nothing to do with it."

Dad smiles. "All of that stuff is man–made," he says pointedly. "You're doing it to yourselves." I get the image of a beautiful planet with all of its physical systems in balance.

"So why is mankind so messed up?" I ask.

He sighs. "If I told you that the situation on planet earth was perfect, would you believe me?"

"No way," I say. "How about if we eliminated war, for starters?"

"War, poverty, all that bad stuff is one of the reasons the earth environment is so powerful and attractive," he says lovingly. "It makes the highs so much higher."

"Try telling that to the billions who live in poverty," I say, irritated. "Conditions for so many of us are appalling."

"Then why are there 6 billion human beings currently on the planet?" dad asks. "If being human is so bad, why are there so many who want to incarnate?"

I think about that for a few minutes. "It's insane," I conclude.

"On one of my tapes (from Abraham) Jerry Hicks asks Abraham what's the point of life from a chicken's perspective. The poor things are thrown in cages and they exist just to be slaughtered and eaten by humans. Abraham responds by saying, 'Then why does the consciousness of the chicken continue to come into chicken bodies?' You said the same thing."

"That's right," he says. "When you reach a full understanding of the system, and how it works, and who you are, you become filled with wonder and joy and passion at the magnificence of it all."

I get the most incredible rush of positive emotion. It's awesome!

'I still don't get it," I say. "You feel so fantastic and by comparison I feel like shit. It's no fair!"

He laughs. "Well," he says, "I can't wait to come back. I want to see if I can do better next time. I want to see if I can truly enjoy myself on earth. So many do, you know."

Now I feel like a failure. "My life has either been complete joyful, or I'm feeling depressed," I say. "I seem to get 8 or 9 years of joy followed by one year in the shithopper, as you used to say to Sue." (Dad always used to tell my sister that everyone has to spend time in the shithopper).

"Your life has been very successful," he says. "You wanted to experience the bad times along with the good. You feel the highs and the lows with excruciating intensity."

"I must have been a moron," I said. "It feels so horrible to feel horrible!"

"That's all a distant memory to me now," dad says, unconcerned. For him, it's all good, and he knows it's all good for me too. That's a point of view I'd like to have all the time.

"Vroom, vroom!" he says. "I think I'll go to the track."

And he's gone.

Reincarnating Back on Earth

The day is very warm and blustery for early November in Michigan. The temperature is in the upper 50's and the wind is gusting to 30 mph. We had high winds on Sunday that knocked our power out for over two days.

I don't feel him at all as I stride out of the driveway and out onto the dirt road in front of the house. I gaze into Merle Kern's field across Northfield Church, a square mile of brown open space with the remnants of this year's soybean crop. The scene reminds me of a nature painting and the electrical lines along Pontiac Trail look as if they have been painted with a line brush. The sun is peeping in and out of the white wisps of clouds that race across the sky. I am almost halfway through when I feel him.

"How are you dad?"

He feels bigger and wiser than ever before. "I AM," he says, accompanied by a feeling of well being. "I'm almost ready to go back to earth."

I can feel it. He seems eager and excited.

I'm a little apprehensive. "I want to be able to talk to you," I say. "I'm really enjoying having a mentor and a father. It's working out real good now that you're dead."

He bursts out laughing. "Yeah, we MacLeans do everything ass–backwards, don't we?"

I'm laughing too. That was one of his favorite expressions when he was alive.

Logically, our conversations aren't happening. A psychiatrist would say that our dialogue is all in my head. Maybe it is, I don't know, but it sure seems real to me.

"You can still talk to me any time you want," dad reminds me.

"How can I talk to you if you go back to earth?"

Instead of explaining, he indicates the sky above. I feel a larger presence, or consciousness, as if only part of me perceives through the body's eyes.

"Not all of you is occupying that body," he confirms.

"Nonsense," I say. "All of me is right here." I feel my feet crunching against the little pebbles along the side of the road as I walk along Earhart, and I can see, in the distance over a mile away, the pine tree that I call the knife tree, along Sutton Road.

In response, he directs my attention around me. "Feel how big you are," and I can sort of feel it, a consciousness or an awareness that seems to be everywhere.

"When you come to earth, the physical experience is so intense and poignant that it drowns out the awareness of your broader self. But the rest of you is still there. You can feel the 'rest' of yourself every time you feel excited, or exhilarated. During those moments, you are literally expanding your awareness to encompass your broader self. "

Wow, that's cool, I think.

Dad feels even less like my father and more like a very powerful being. Almost like a god. Or God. I'm sure that's why Neale Donald Walsch entitles his series of dialogues 'Conversations with God.' I used to think that was pretentious, but not anymore.

Dad is a lot different now, but I like him a lot better.

"So part of you goes into the body and the rest of you stays outside it?" I ask. I'm having a hard time thinking of people being able to split themselves up.

Dad laughs. "As you spend more and more "time" here, you become more aware of the Oneness of universal consciousness," he says. "But that's not necessarily the greatest thing. The main reason for the existence of the physical universe is to maintain, and even increase, the existence of separate personalities."

"Explain."

"Well, the more I'm here the more I understand things. On earth it's just the opposite. On earth you are forced to make decisions. The tendency is to become separated, more isolated. But the great advantage is that you become more and more opinionated, more and more individualistic."

"Isn't that bad?" I ask. "On earth we need more harmony, not less!"

"Depends on you point of view son," he says lovingly. "I long for that individualistic feeling of being myself, separate, an utterly unique personality like no other."

"But you already said that you don't lose awareness of who you are when you die. In fact, you said that you become more aware of yourself," I object.

"That's right," he acknowledges. "But the assumption of a physical perspective strengthens the whole. The One wants to experience Itself in as many ways as it possibly can. That is why we have created a practically infinite universe of physical experience. I can only say that there is absolutely nothing like a physical incarnation. It is the most real, poignant experience you can possibly have. Even though I have complete freedom here, and have my choice of an infinite smorgasbord of places to go and things to do, there's something lacking."

I think of my favorite channel, Esther Hicks, and Abraham. "Abraham is a collective consciousness," dad says. "For some in native state, it's easier to combine consciousness to get that unique viewpoint. On earth, the physical body provides a built–in separation. Earth is like an identity generator."

"I'm not sure I understand."

"There's so much crap out there, you are forced to make up your mind about what you like and what you don't. That automatically enhances and strengthens your individual point of view."

(Dad says, "Don't write 'crap' in the above sentence. You're putting words in my mouth. It's not bad, it just is. Write, 'variety.'" I stick out my tongue. "It's my book, and I say it's crap." He laughs, and I grin. "I can finally get the last word, ha–ha!" This is so cool, I think. Kenneth MacLean Sr. always had to have control. Now he's as cheerful as a little kid splashing around in the bathtub.)

"The physical body is vulnerable," he says. "On earth there is the idea that when your physical body is dead, you are gone forever. Up here, we're mostly just play acting in our adventures. On earth, you can feel excruciating pain. You can die. Now we're talking about a game that's for keeps. When you bungee jump off that bridge, there's the possibility of a horrible outcome. You see horrific outcomes every day on the news. The idea is, 'it could happen to you too!' But all of this lends zest and exhilaration to the experience that you just can't get in native state. That's why I never want earth to change. There are plenty of planets you can incarnate on if you want to experience peace and harmony. But there are very few places like earth. Some of us are addicted to it, as I said before."

Wow.

Dad drifts off. As I walk along Northfield Church I begin to think about the body I got this time around. As my doctor told me 25 years ago when I was having heart trouble, "Let's just say that you didn't get the strongest constitution." He knows iridology, which says that the condition of your internal organs can be detected by looking in the iris of the eye. A strong body will have lots of fine white lines radiating out from the pupil. I have been noticing the irises of the various people I meet lately when I talk with them. All of them have beautiful, bright, unblemished blue eyes. When I look in the mirror, I see a lot of darkness. I shouldn't be surprised, I think. Mom died of cancer at 29, grandpa was only 50 when he had his fatal heart attack, and mom's dad died of a heart attack at 53… Dad interrupts my train of thought. "That's unproductive," he says. He reminds me of that early childhood incident that has seemed to define my life psychologically (the time I went into my parents' bedroom when they were having sex). "You decided right there that it was a bad thing to be you," he points out.

In my mind there is an explosion of awareness. "That's right!" I exclaim. "But it was your fault!"

He is unapologetic. "No son," he says. "Just because you have a tiny body doesn't mean you aren't making decisions, and in charge of what decisions you make."

I am sputtering and fuming but for the first time I really understand what he's saying. I am almost home, and I begin to feel a sense of peace and calm. "So I have completely created my life. Only me, nobody else."

"Yes," he says lovingly. "There aren't any victims. You always get to choose. The people in your life just give you the opportunity to choose."

I'm going to have to think about that. It still seems to me that big people have an inordinate influence over children.

Every Human Being is a Master

On my CD player the Latin sounds of "Tumba Palo Cocuye" from the Afro-Cuban All-Stars fills the air, and I am tapping my feet. I have no idea what these cats are saying, but the music is incredible. Dad hated anything that wasn't classical music, or the Kingston Trio, but he likes this stuff. "I missed out on a lot of enjoyment last time around," he says. "Next time it's going to be different."

"How do you know?" I tease.

He smiles. "That's the exciting part. I haven't got a clue how it's going to turn out."

"Then why go?" I ask. "Stay in joy and save yourself a lot of misery."

It's clear that he has no intention of following my advice. "You know what I miss the most about earth?" he asks.

"Sex?"

He laughs. "No, what I miss the most is just the feel of being in a body. There's nothing like it."

"But you said before that you can experience through our eyes," I say.

"Yes, that's true," he says. "But I'll tell you a little secret. Those of you living on earth are the true masters. So many of you look up to your channels, your spirits speaking through human voices, and wish, 'Oh, if only I could be like them!' Well son, when you 'die' and find out what the score is (another of dad's favorite sayings), you'll understand that we learn far more from you than you ever learn from us. Take your Abraham, for instance. One of their favorite sayings is 'If we were in your physical shoes, we'd do (blah–blah).' I have some news for you: Abraham doesn't choose to experience physically. So they don't truly know what it's like on earth from a human perspective. They're inspirational and wonderful and what they say is true. But don't look up to them. Every one of you, even the drunken bum living in a box, is powerful beyond your understanding. You are the Masters, every one of you. Believe me, when you get here you are going to cherish every one of your uncomfortable and painful moments. Every experience you have had and are going to have as a human being is a precious jewel. Every event in your life contributes to the strengthening of your personality, and to the understanding of the One, and contributes many more notes to the symphony of life and the expansion of consciousness."

Dad is passionate and enraptured.

"When you return from your life on earth, it takes you a while to find your feet. You're so used to having the body filter your perception for you, that you forget you have the power to create what you perceive and what you experience. Here, there is a wonderful feeling of 'we are all in this together.' That is something I really miss when I'm on earth, I have to admit. But the poignancy of the earth experience makes up for all that."

"I'd think you might have just gotten sick of earth," I say.

"Yes, I did," he says reflectively. "I was weary beyond belief. But I was taught that it was my obligation to live as long as I could. On earth, life is a contest to see who can live the longest, when it is really a personal decision for each being. You might only want to take a few breaths in a human body, and then decide to leave (crib death). Or you might have accomplished your life goals as a young man and decide to leave. Or you might feel trapped and decide that it's pointless to continue. That's how 'accidents' happen. The teenage daughter involved in a fatal car crash (Dad gets this from an actual event in my mind) has decided that she's had it, and so she meets up with the guy who falls asleep at the wheel, careens over the guard rail and hits her head–on."

I stop for now, and pick this up three days later. Again, dad is right there with me again.

"When are you going to return to earth?" I ask.

"I already have," he says. "I'm living all of the lives I've ever lived right now, and I'm planning the ones I'm going to live as well."

"I don't understand," I reply. "You can't live all lifetimes at the same time."

"Well there you go with time again," he says. "I'm aware of all the physical experiences I've ever had. I can relive anything that ever happened to me anytime I want. In that sense, I am living all of my lifetimes right now."

"But it's not the same," I say. "You can't say that a lifetime you had in 1000BC is the same as your last one."

"But it is," he says. "Remember, the consciousness that incarnates is only an aspect of your greater self. There is not a one–to–one correspondence of consciousness with physical bodies. I am at the same time existing in every physical lifetime I have ever had, and aware of the fullness of myself. It's something you won't get until you pass away and fully find yourself."

Wow. That's heavy–duty stuff. I admit I don't really get it. But I understand from what he sends me that HE gets it. I just feel that it makes perfect sense to him, even though I can't put it into words very well.

"If time is meaningless then you should be able to read the future until the end of the universe," I say. "So what point is there in living if you already know what happens?"

He smiles. "We can't predict the future, and the universe is eternal, never–ending. Just as you aren't sure exactly what you will do tomorrow in every detail, it is the same with me."

OK, I think. I'll let that pass. But of course he is aware of my thoughts, so I can't put anything past him. If I ever could. "You know son, I have more control over you now than I ever did," he says, reading my mind. "You thought I was a control freak on earth!" He goes off laughing and laughing like a little kid.

I can feel that he regards my problems as utterly trivial. There is a feeling of complete well–being from him and a complete certainty that all is perfect.

I never got to ask him where he decided to incarnate. I don't really believe what he's saying about that anyway. How can you live in a body on earth and at the same time be floating around in heaven? I guess it all depends on your perspective. From my point of view here on earth, it seems that life after death is a lot easier and more rewarding. Dad was often a miserable bastard on earth, but he has the last laugh now.

The Circle of Life: Becoming a Baby Once More

It's funny. Dad isn't as strong a presence as he was before. Could it be that he really did go back to earth? I asked him that.

"Well, you don't 'lose' awareness because a part of you goes to earth. But I have to say that the earth experience is so stimulating and exciting that most of my attention is there now. Maybe that's why you don't feel me as strongly. But I'm still here for you."

"OK, so where are you now? What family and environment did you choose?"

In response, he sends me some images, but since I'm seeing them through a baby's eyes, all I get is a jumble. "Sorry about that," he says. "I'm just getting used to a new body again. I can't stay in there for any length of time."

Well, if you thought I was weird before, you're probably ready to put me in a straight jacket! Here I am talking to my "father" who is now a baby? It seems weird even to me!

"So where are you?" I ask. Just as he is about to answer, the little chipmunk who is living in our house (to the great frustration of our two cats) makes a noise from the back of my office. The little guy can squeeze himself into such small spaces that we can't catch him. Dad laughs. "Who do you think that chipmunk is?" he says.

"What do you mean? He's just a cute little rodent," I respond.

"That rodent has the consciousness of your grandma Martin," he says. "Remember her? She always thought you were something special."

This is getting too strange. "Excuse me, but that chipmunk is just a scruffy little animal."

"Remember that consciousness isn't limited, like physical matter," he replies. "There are billions of animals and insects on earth — how do you think that happens?"

I am blown away. It's almost enough to make me believe in the biological basis for consciousness — you know, the "man is meat" theory that says who you are is just a bunch of neurons firing in a mass of protoplasm called the brain. That would explain everything very nicely. Dad guffaws. "When you die you're dead?' he exclaims. "It doesn't work that way."

"So every animal has a separate conscious personality?' I ask. This is getting a little uncomfortable.

"You still don't understand," he says, "for all of the books you write and that website you have. Look," he says, pointing a metaphorical finger at me. "I can be two places at once, or three, or four, or a whole lot more. I can experience separately from each of these physical points of view, without losing touch with ME."

"I'm sorry," I say, a little exasperated. "I don't get it. I'm ME too, but I don't feel anybody else! I'm a separate personality from my 'higher self' or my 'past lives' or whatever you want to call it."

"That's because you don't really know what the score is," he says smugly. "You always thought you were so smart, but I'm a lot brighter than you now. So why don't you listen to your old man for once?" Well, that feels like Kenneth MacLean Sr. all right. He is smiling, sort of tongue–in–cheek.

"I'm glad you're having fun with it," I say, "because it sounds like a lot of hooey to me." I say this even though I know what he's saying is true, at least for HIM. I can feel it. But I'm frustrated because I can't really get it. I feel like a physicist who is confronted by a new–ager who tells him that she can see auras, and when he asks her to show him an aura and she can't, he says, "If you can't observe it, it's not true." I suppose it's not important anyway. The main thing is that I know my father is really happy. But I feel I'm losing touch with him. He's getting spread around too thin for my taste.

Dad laughs again. "I'm still here," he says. "But I'm not so fond of the personality I was when I was Kenneth MacLean Sr. So I've mostly let go of that."

That's not such a bad thing, I think. I wasn't so fond of him either!

I want to ask him more questions about where his new body is.

"That's really important to you, isn't it?" he asks.

"Well yeah! I've heard that if you were a male in one lifetime in the U.S. you might be a female in China the next."

He smiles. "Right now I have a male body," he says. "I didn't do very well last time as a father, so I'm going to try again." As I write all this I wonder what my sister Sue is thinking. She reads this stuff, and probably thinks I've gone bonkers.

"I'm losing contact," he says. "You're too much into self doubt now to continue this conversation."

It's all my fault again, I guess. As the oldest child, I felt I got blamed for a lot of stuff that wasn't my fault.

Oh well, maybe I'll try him again tomorrow.

The Vortex

It's a beautiful day today, and warmer, so I decide to go out for a walk. The past week was a typical Michigan late November day: a slate gray sky, temperature in the twenties and thirties (and teens at night), and a fairly strong wind. But today the sun is out.

As I begin my walk I think about how strange my life is. As I mentioned before, since the age of 18, I have enjoyed 8 or 9 years of perfect health and happiness, followed by a year or more in the shithopper, as dad used to say. This year of 2005 has been one of my down years, but even so I have experienced a lot of growth. In fact, although I wouldn't want to have to go through it again, I have made great strides in my understanding of myself and life.

As I stride along the dirt road with the sun in my face and the breeze at my back, I can feel Dad again. He's enjoying himself, looking through my eyes. Our last conversation was a little bizarre, I thought, and after I wondered whether I had made it all up.

I say to him, "OK, if you're really real and I'm not making this all up, show me how I'm messing up my energy." I believe firmly that the causes of negative emotion and even physiological conditions have their root within the human consciousness. If Dad is really a spirit and can see me as I really am, then he should be able to 'diagnose' my problem. I give him permission to do so (I never trusted him when he was alive, but it's different now).

After a few seconds, I feel a sort of twisting. It starts about 3 feet on top of my head and goes right through the middle of my body, and goes down even below my feet, somewhat like a tornado funnel.

"What the heck?" I think, concerned that I might have encountered some negative or evil entity. He smiles.

"It's all right son," dad says. "You wanted me to show you what you're doing, and I'm showing you." On a sideband he thinks, 'This guy is very sensitive.' These sidebands of thought, from the former policeman and running back, go something like, 'kind of a sissy, isn't he? It's no wonder I never understood him.' Sometimes I think I pick up on his former incarnation. If it's true what Abraham says, that thoughts maintain their existence, then the personality that was Kenneth MacLean Sr. still exists somewhere in the ethers. That would go a long way to explaining the presence of 'evil spirits.' When I am fully connected with the source of my father, all I feel are positive vibes. The idea of protecting yourself from evil entities then becomes a futile exercise. All of this passes through my mind in about a nanosecond, as I feel the twisting energy like a tornado funnel, contracting my energy uncomfortably. Dad says, "That's what you're doing."

"Just go with it, "he says, "don't be afraid. It's the fear of something that actually creates the condition you fear.

It's hard to describe what's happening. The twisting feels like I'm in the middle of a vortex that is moving faster and faster, and I'm feeling squashed and turned inside out. All of a sudden I feel an explosion of energy, and become aware of a spherical/toroidal field of energy surrounding me, expanding. It's kind of like the computer animation I programmed in the article on my website. I begin to feel much better.

"I don't like the going inward," I say. "It feels much better to expand."

"No son," he says. "You have to accept, and have the ability, to both go inward and outward."

Wow. I couldn't have made this up. I can actually feel the vortex through the middle of my body, and the expansion of my energy outward. It's pretty cool.

"Is there really a toroidal field of energy surrounding the human body?" I ask.

He smiles. "We're using the analogies you understand," he says.

"Yes, but is it really like that?" I insist.

He explodes into laughter. "By God," he says, "could there have been two more opposite people than you or I?" Dad was not an intellectual, to say the least. I feel a little release from him, as if he has now understood his former personality a lot better. "No wonder we didn't get along so well!" Even though we talked on the phone every week, Dad and I did very well separated by 2,600 miles of distance.

Now he tells me to twist inward, and I'm a little afraid. I don't like how it feels. "Go ahead," he says. "You have to be able to consciously manipulate your energy field." I twist inward and it doesn't feel right, but I do it anyway. I feel like I'm going down the rabbit hole, into a dark abyss. Then, just as I feel assort of black singularity beneath my feet, the energy explodes outward. Clockwise seems to contract, and counter–clockwise to expand.

"Now do the exercise and make counter–clockwise contract, and clockwise expand." I do it, and it feels pretty cool.

"Now have the energy come up from your feet and exit at the top of your head." I do that, and I'm feeling pretty loose. I'm not sure whether the readers should try this at home. It's pretty powerful stuff.

"Satisfied that I'm real now?" he jokes.

"Yeah, I guess I am," I say, amazed. Dad feels a lot more like me than him. He laughs again. "You and I are so alike," he says, contradicting himself. "It's amazing that we were so different on earth."

Yeah, it is amazing, but it's a little depressing too. It would have been nice to have a real dad, not someone who criticized me all the time.

"Cheer up!" he says. "It takes two to tango, kid," reminding me that I'm not a victim, and that our life together was a co–creation. "That sort of thinking will just spin you in," he says wisely.

I smile. "I guess it's OK," I say. "You feel like a father to me now and a mentor as well.

Dad is pleased.

My life is amazing, I think. Either that, or I'm just a little twisted.

Dad hushes me. "Enough of that…" he whispers, and he's gone.

Heavenly Advice

I've been feeling too tired to walk much lately. Haven't felt dad around much. I kind of miss him.

"I've been hanging around with Norma a lot (my step-mom)," he says. "She's starting to open up a little."

"But you're a spirit now," I say. "You should be able to be in two places at once."

He laughs. "That's right son," he says. "But I've decided that you should be on your own from now on."

That upsets me. "You weren't there for me when you were alive, now it's the same story when you're dead!"

"It's about time you stopped worrying about what I said to you, or did to you, or how other people think of you. That has been a big problem in your life. You need to come out of your shell."

I am about to say that I have published two books and a website, but I think I know what he means. "You mean, stop hiding your light under a bushel and get out in front of people. Something you never did your whole life," I object.

"That's right!" he says cheerfully. "But I don't have to deal with that anymore because I'm dead. You do. I can tell you right now that you need to work on your presentation and just get up there and deliver it. It will be the best thing that ever happened to you."

"I'm taking voice lessons right now," I say.

"I know you are," he says. "But you're still not committed to speaking in front of people. You need to do it, even if it's scary for you."

OK dad. "Do as I say, not as I do," I respond.

"You can't hurt me or razz me," he says. "I was always too strong for you when I was alive, and now I feel so great I don't care what you say or think about me."

I know he's right. "It's just that the stuff I'm offering is kinda out there," I say.

He laughs. "What you're saying is the truth. It doesn't matter how many fundamentalists or skeptics disagree with you. Consciousness is eternal, there IS life after death, and you know it, so stop f—ing around. You made a good start with your books but you can reach more people by speaking. So just go and do it!"

Well, I think, first I have to figure out what I'm going to say, then I have to advertise and promote...

"There you go again, putting things off," he says. "I did that my whole life and I just contracted into myself more and more. The same thing is already happening to you. Why do you think you've suffered those bouts of depression? You had the idea when you arrived that you'd change the world with spiritual knowledge, but you've always been afraid to speak your truth. You are part of a very large group of people who came into this life with that idea. Most of you have done nothing with your knowledge from native state, and have just blended in to the crowd. You and those like you have allowed the domineering, controlling people to take power. You have a strong connection to us (the spirit world). Trust yourself. Don't let yourself down, or others who are waiting to hear the truth. The truth about Spirit can never be repeated often enough. You need to shout it from the rooftops and be dammed to anyone who objects, do you understand?"

Dad has never been so forceful. He always thought I was full of it when he was alive, and was not bashful in expressing that idea to me.

"I didn't get it when I was alive," he said. "I lost my connection to my greater self. But you haven't. It's your responsibility to tell the world what you know."

I have to admit that I'm intimidated speaking in front of people. But I can feel that he's right. So I guess I'll have to continue on the path.

"You won't regret it,' he says. "Go for it, and don't look back."

I get the idea of a guy on a tightrope. When he looks down he gets scared, but when he looks forward and moves forward, he retains his balance.

"Go for it son," he whispers. "Don't be afraid…"

The Power of Consciousness

Dad seems to be in the background these days. I don't know whether that's because I haven't been thinking much about him lately, or because he's gone off to do other things.

"I'm still here," he says. "You haven't needed me, so I haven't been present for you."

It's good to feel his energy again. My father was (is) really a great guy. Too bad he didn't often express his true self when he was alive.

He's giving me all sorts of stuff but I'm too slow typing to keep up with him. Basically he says, "You haven't been so hot at that yourself," then he sticks out his tongue and laughs. In my human form I can't understand how anyone can change so quickly. He's a wise old man, then he's a young man feeling his oats, then he's a kid. His various aspects seem to come in all at once and then I have to translate that into words. It's like—BAM! A whole package of thoughts and feelings all rolled up into what feels like an impulse. It's what intuition, or inspiration feels like. It's pretty cool.

I wonder if that's how non-corporeal spirits communicate, and he gets enthusiastic. "Oh yes, it's wonderful! I can say anything I want, knowing I will never be misunderstood. I can't tell you what a relief that is for me."

He wants me to change "say" to "communicate."

"Speech is such a limited form of expression," he says. "Compared to my capabilities now, it's doesn't convey hardly anything."

"So what are you doing now?" I ask.

"Well, a part of me is in a body on earth again, and it's a lot of fun perceiving through those physical eyes."

I still don't get how a part of you can be in a body and a part of you not. I get this crystal clear image of a baby lying in a crib and Dad having the ability to enter and exit the body at will. Dad is so much MORE than just the little baby body; in fact, he's a really big being that is having fun with his physical aspect. I don't know how to communicate this other than to say that the "Higher Self" IS the person, and the perception through the body is just an aspect of a much broader awareness. "Remember that the body has awareness too, on a cellular level," Dad says. "A physical incarnation is a cooperative effort."

It's so cool to be able to talk to the old man like this. I never could when he was just "dad."

"I'm totally cool now," he says. "I'm with it, and I know all the lingo." I laugh. He looks like a beatnik in baggy clothes, a goatee, and a cigarette hanging from his mouth. "You crack me up dad." I'm laughing. "You're only 50 years behind the times."

"Hah!" he says. "I'm all a dat', homeslice."

"Ok dad." I'm smiling. I can feel him all around me, and it's a really great feeling. I know I can reach him whenever I want, even after a couple of weeks of not giving him a thought.

"That's right," he says. "Time isn't an impediment up here. Visit any time you want. You don't need a car, or a password, or an internet connection. That's the power of being, the power of consciousness."

Dad's pretty smart, I have to admit.

He laughs. "Not bad for an old man, eh?"

Not bad at all, I think. "I love you dad."

"I love you too."

Love transcends pitiful barriers like physical bodies. I wish everyone could communicate with their parents like this. If people understood what they're really capable of, we could transform our societies almost overnight.

A New Life

It's been a week since I talked with Dad. I don't feel him very strongly at all — it's like his attention is very focused on something else.

"I am really into my new life on earth," he says.

Apparently, the physical universe is like a drug for some of us -- even though all of dad isn't in his new body, it seems as if all of his attention is there. "Yeah!" he says. "It's fun being a little baby again!"

Like a little child at play, he doesn't have a lot of attention on me anymore. That makes me a little sad, but he says, "You can always get my attention anytime you want. But you have to be clear and ask with intent. I've completely let go of my previous life and I'm on to the future!! Yay!!!" he says enthusiastically.

I can tell that this will be the end of these conversations.

"I've told you everything you need to know," Dad says. "Have fun. Live! And don't look back. Believe me, everything is perfect. When you return, you'll know that without the slightest doubt, but don't wait around for that to happen. Create your own heaven on earth."

What have I learned from these conversations? That consciousness lives on. That each one of us is divine and eternal. And I understand that my dad is happy, wherever he is. That's the most important thing of all.

~~~ THE END ~~~

About the Author

Kenneth J. M. MacLean is a spiritual author who has written eight books and written dozens of articles. He has produced two films: *The Unity of Spirit and Matter* and *The Law Of Attraction Explained*.

For free articles, eBooks, movies, and more, you are invited to visit Ken's personal web site:

http://www.kjmaclean.com.

Expand your consciousness
with these other great titles by K.J.M. MacLean!

Visit www.KJMaclean.com to preview or purchase!

www.ingramcontent.com/pod-product-compliance
Lightning Source LLC
Chambersburg PA
CBHW021019090426
42738CB00007B/827